glee for Ukulele

Music From The FOX Television Show

ISBN 978-1-4234-9616-8

HAL•LEONARD®
CORPORATION
7777 W. BLUEMOUND RD. P.O. BOX 13819 MILWAUKEE, WI 53213

Visit Hal Leonard Online at
www.halleonard.com

Bad Romance

Words and Music by Stefani Germanotta and Nadir Khayat

First note

Intro
Moderate Techno

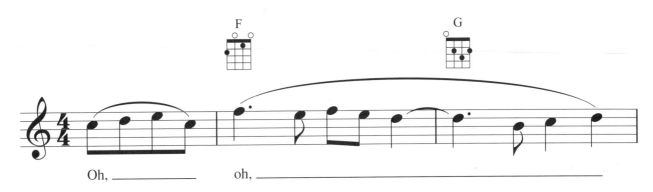

Oh, _____ oh, _____

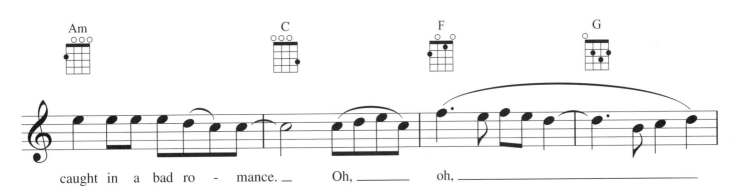

caught in a bad ro - mance. ___ Oh, _____ oh, _____

Refrain

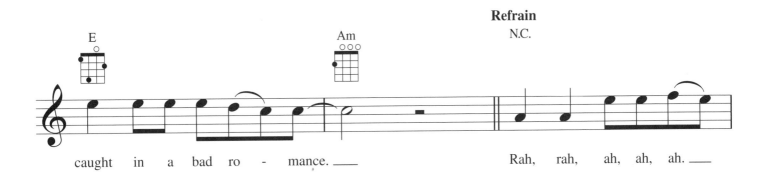

caught in a bad ro - mance. ___ Rah, rah, ah, ah, ah. ___

Ro - ma, ro - ma, ma. ___ Ga - ga, ooh, la, la. ___ Want your bad ro - mance.

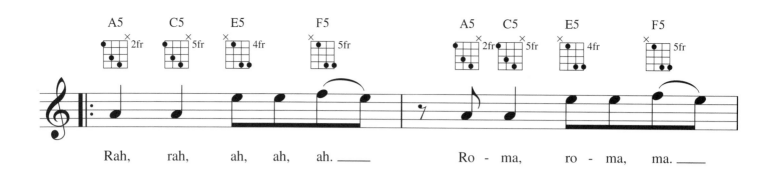

Rah, rah, ah, ah, ah. _____ Ro - ma, ro - ma, ma. _____

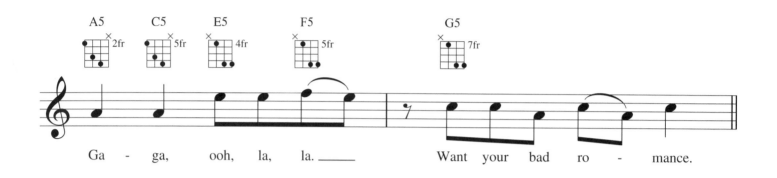

Ga - ga, ooh, la, la. _____ Want your bad ro - mance.

Verse

1. I want your ug - ly, I want your dis - ease. _____
2. I want your hor - ror, I want your de - sign _____

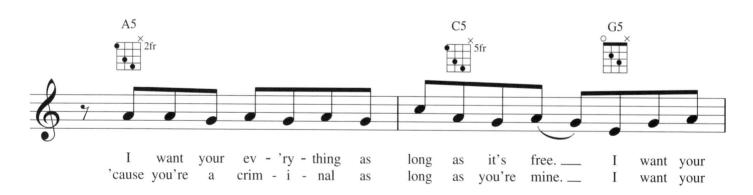

I want your ev - 'ry - thing as long as it's free. ___ I want your
'cause you're a crim - i - nal as long as you're mine. ___ I want your

love.   Love, love, love, I want your love.
love.   Love, love, love, I want your love.

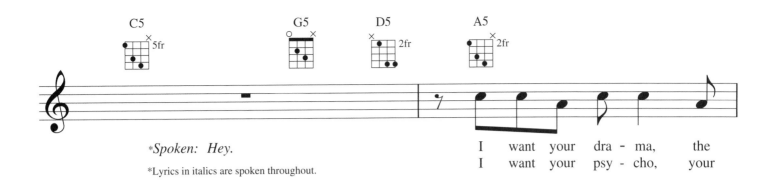

Spoken: Hey.

Lyrics in italics are spoken throughout.

I want your dra - ma, the
I want your psy - cho, your

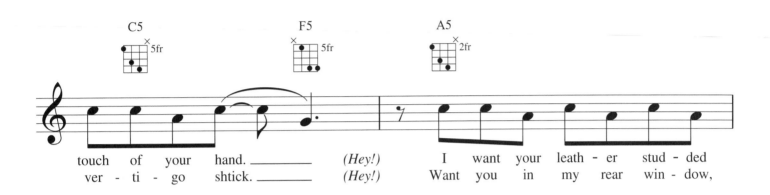

touch of your hand. _____ (Hey!)
ver - ti - go shtick. _____ (Hey!)

I want your leath - er stud - ded
Want you in my rear win - dow,

kiss in the sand. _ I want your love.
ba - by, your sick. _ I want your love.

Love, love, love, I want your

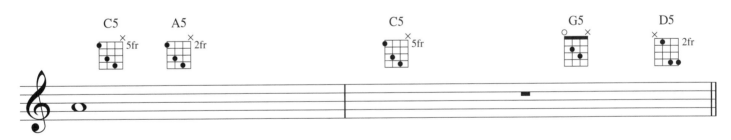

love.

Pre-Chorus

You know that I want_____ you,

5

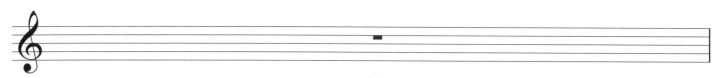

and you know that I need ___ you.

I want it bad, bad ro - mance. ___

𝄋 Chorus

I want your love and I want your re - venge, ___ you and me ___

___ could write a bad ro - mance. ___ Oh, _____ I want your love and all your

lov - in's re - venge, ___ you and me _____ could write a bad ro - mance. ___

___ Oh, _____ oh, _____

caught in a bad ro - mance. ___ Oh, ___ oh, ___

To Coda ⊕

___ caught in a bad ro - mance. ___

Refrain

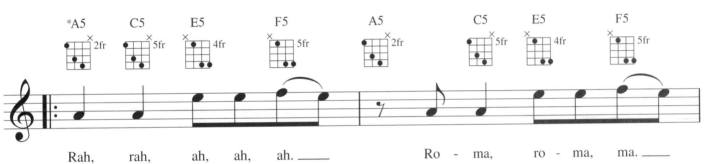

Rah, rah, ah, ah, ah. ___ Ro - ma, ro - ma, ma. ___

*Chord symbols reflect implied harmony, next 4 meas.

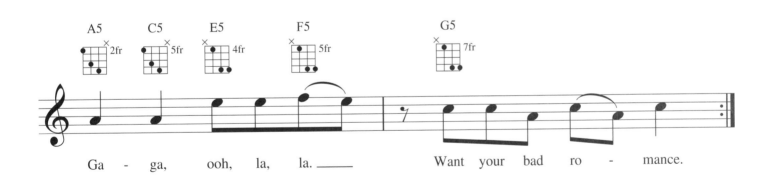

Ga - ga, ooh, la, la. ___ Want your bad ro - mance.

Bridge

Walk, walk, fash - ion ba - by. Work it, move that bitch, c - ra - zy.

1.

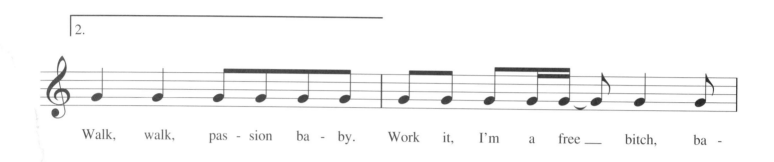

Walk, walk, fash - ion ba - by. Work it, move that bitch, c - ra - zy.

2.

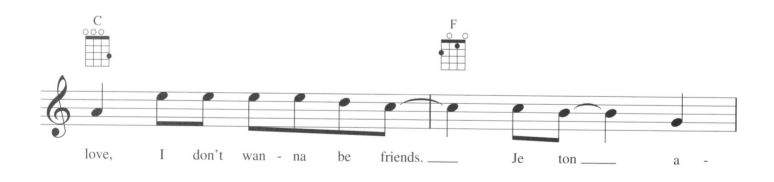

Walk, walk, pas - sion ba - by. Work it, I'm a free ___ bitch, ba -

| F | G | Am |

by. I want ___ your love and I want your re - venge. ___ I want ___ your

| C | F |

love, I don't wan - na be friends. ____ Je ton ____ a -

| G | E |

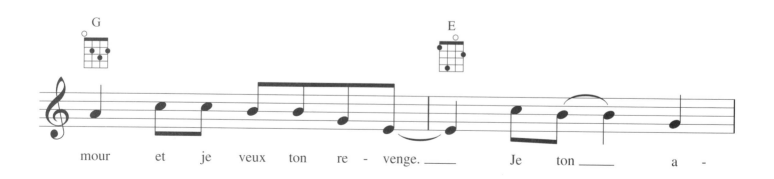

mour et je veux ton re - venge. ____ Je ton ____ a -

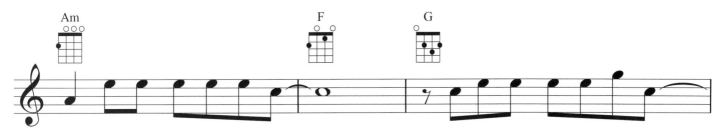

mour.   I   don't   wan - na   be   friends. __   No,   I   don't   wan - na   be   friends. __

__   I   don't   wan - na   be   friends. _____

D.S. al Coda

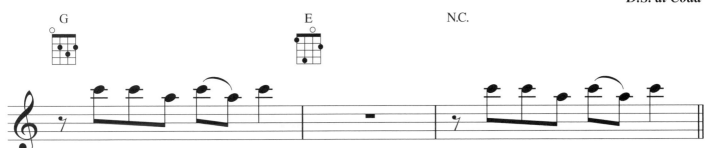

Want   your   bad   ro - mance.   Want   your   bad   ro - mance.

Coda

Outro-Refrain

N.C.

Rah,   rah,   ah,   ah,   ah. ____   Ro - ma,   ro - ma,   ma. ____

Ga - ga,   ooh,   la,   la. ____   Want   your   bad   ro - mance.

Beautiful

Words and Music by Linda Perry

First note

Intro
Moderately slow

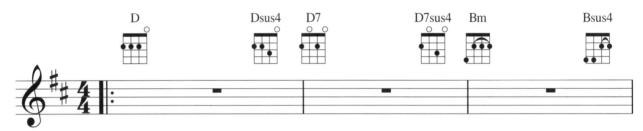

*Whispered: Don't look at me.
*1st time only.

Verse

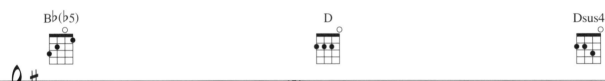

1. Ev - 'ry day is so
2. To all your friends, you're de -

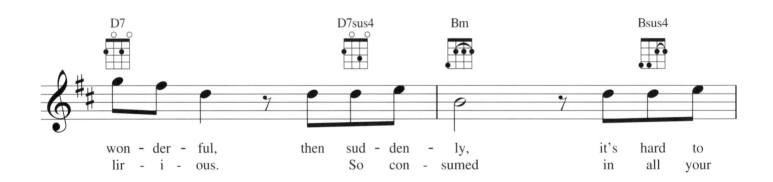

won - der - ful, then sud - den - ly, it's hard to
lir - i - ous. So con - sumed in all your

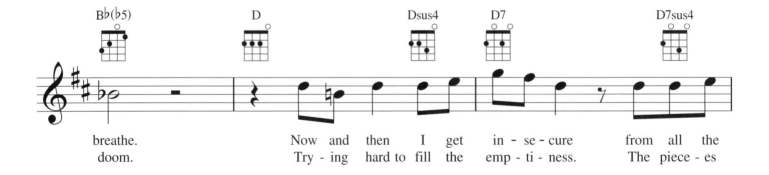

breathe. Now and then I get in - se - cure from all the
doom. Try - ing hard to fill the emp - ti - ness. The piec - es

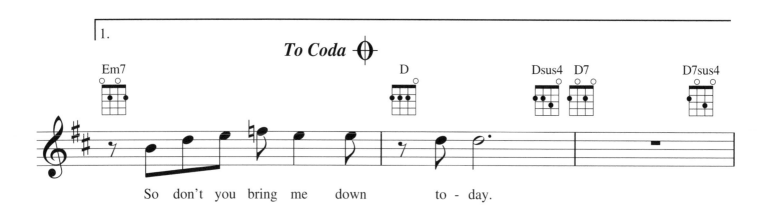

So don't you bring me down to - day.

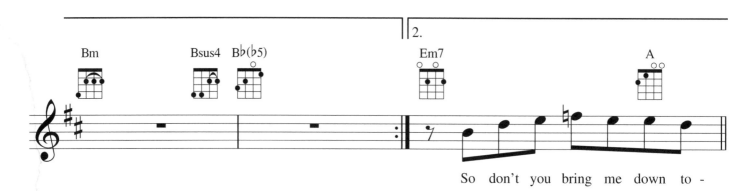

So don't you bring me down to -

Bridge

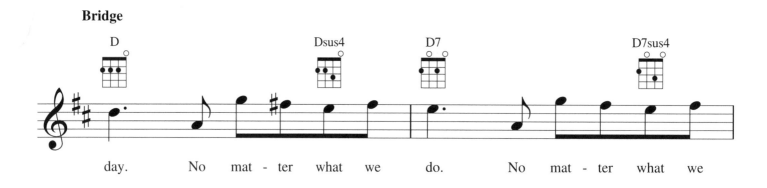

day.   No - mat - ter what we   do.   No - mat - ter what we

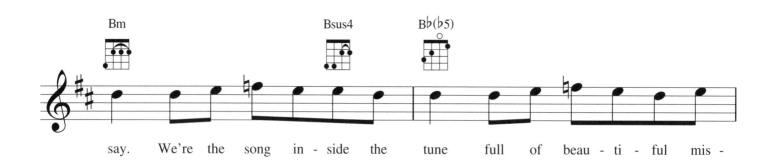

say.   We're the song in - side the   tune   full of beau - ti - ful mis -

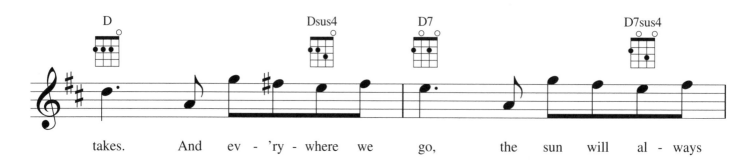

takes.   And ev - 'ry - where we   go,   the sun will al - ways

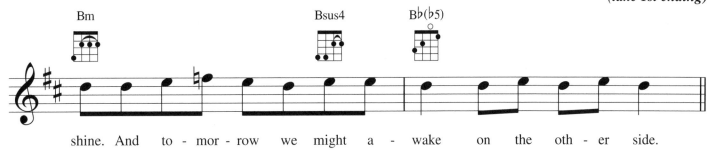

shine. And to-mor-row we might a - wake on the oth - er side.

⊕ Coda

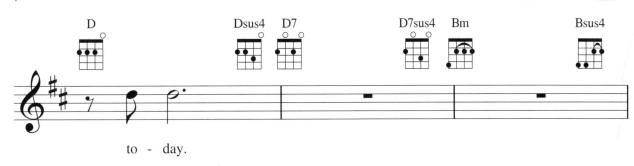

to - day.

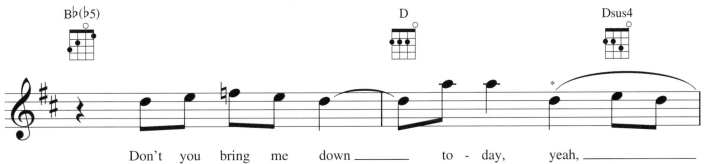

Don't you bring me down _____ to - day, yeah, _____

*Sung one octave higher,
next 2 1/2 meas.

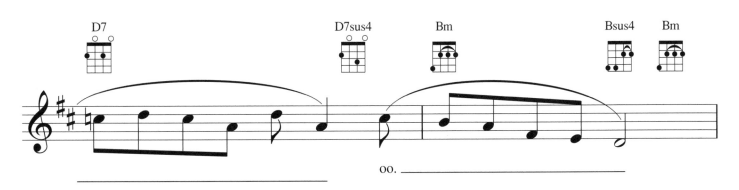

_____ oo. _____

Freely

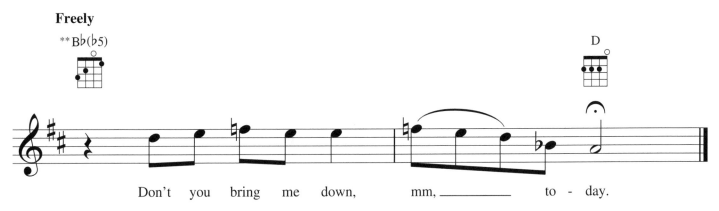

Don't you bring me down, mm, _____ to - day.

**Let chord ring.

Dancing with Myself

Words and Music by Billy Idol and Tony James

To Coda

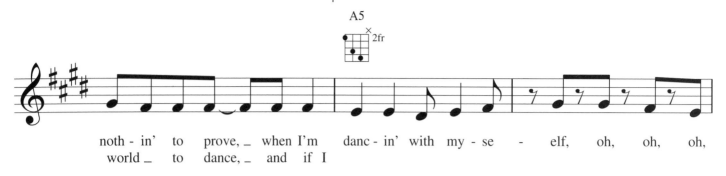

noth - in' to prove, _ when I'm danc - in' with my - se - elf, oh, oh, oh,
world _ to dance, _ and if I

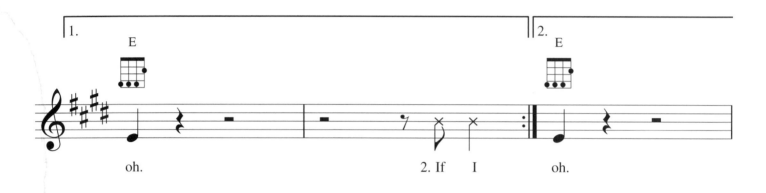

oh. 2. If I oh.

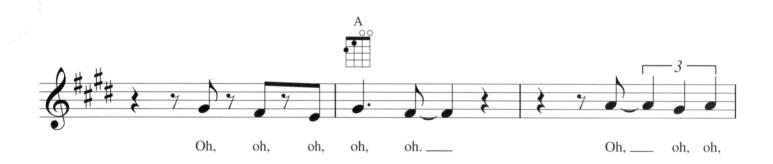

Oh, oh, oh, oh, oh. _____ Oh, _____ oh, oh,

oh, _____ oh, _ oh, oh, oh. _____

Interlude

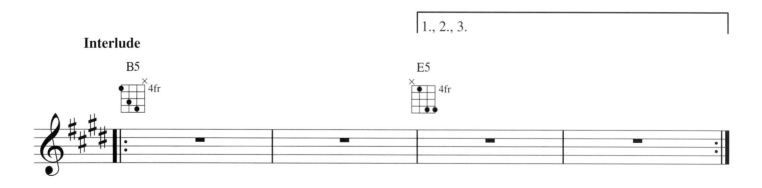

D.S. al Coda

 Coda

3. Well, ___ if I

had __ the chance, __ I'd ask the

world __ to dance. __ If I had ___ the chance, __ I'd ask the

world __ to dance. _____ Oh, oh, oh,

Outro

E5 4fr   A5 2fr

oh.   Oh, oh, oh, oh.   Oh, oh, { oh, / oh. }

w/ Lead Voc. ad lib.

E5 4fr

(Danc - in' with my - se - elf. Oh, oh, oh,

A5 2fr   *Repeat and fade*

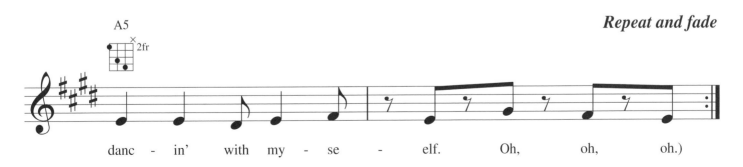

danc - in' with my - se - elf. Oh, oh, oh.)

Defying Gravity

from the Broadway Musical WICKED
Music and Lyrics by Stephen Schwartz

First note

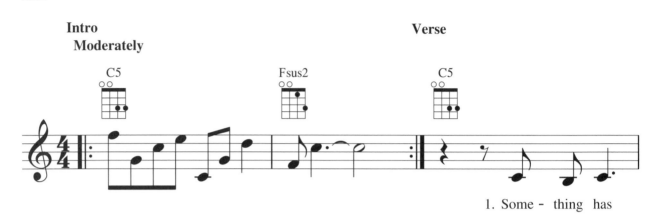

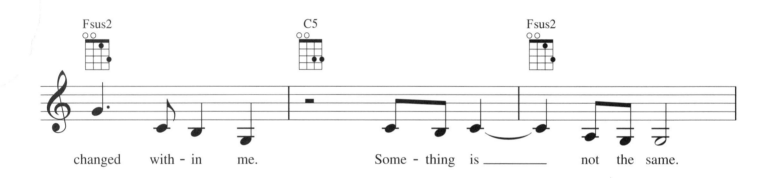

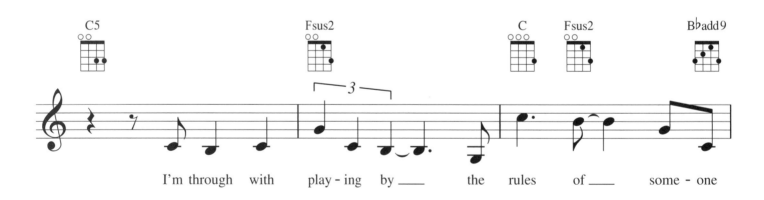

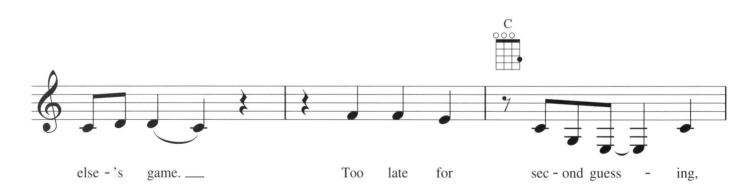

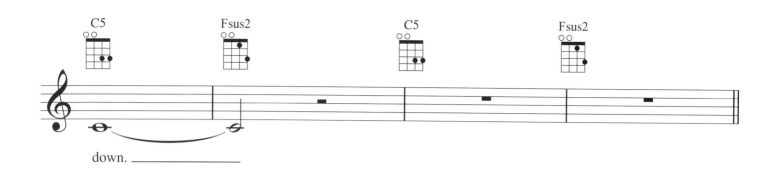

down. _____

Verse

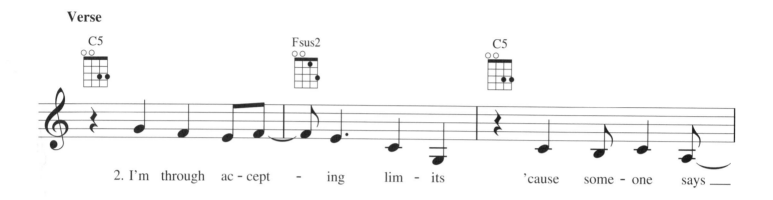

2. I'm through ac-cept - ing lim - its 'cause some - one says ___

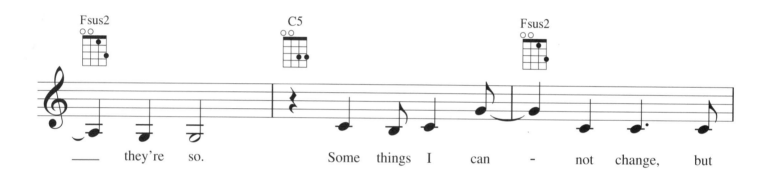

___ they're so. Some things I can - not change, but

'til I try ___ I'll ___ nev - er know. ___ Too long I've ___ been a - fraid of

los - ing love ___ I guess ___ I've lost. Well, if ___ that's

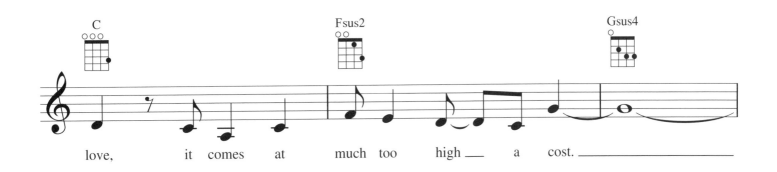

love, it comes at much too high __ a cost. _____

D.S. al Coda 1

⊕ Coda 1

D.S. al Coda 2

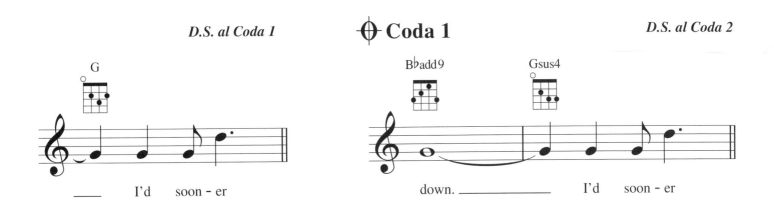

__ I'd soon - er

down. _____ I'd soon - er

⊕ Coda 2

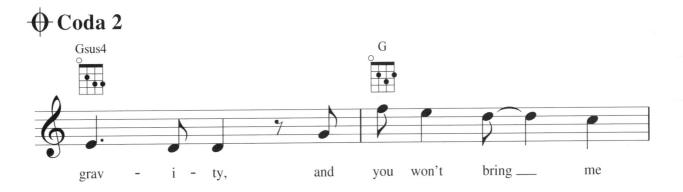

grav - i - ty, and you won't bring __ me

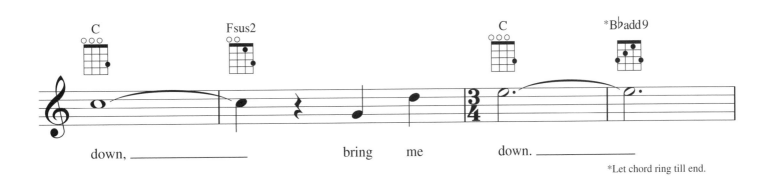

down, _____ bring me down. _____

*Let chord ring till end.

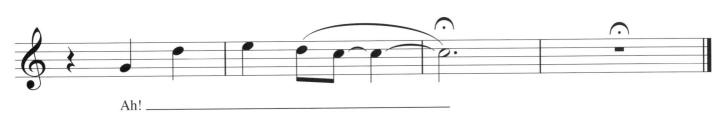

Ah! _____

Don't Rain on My Parade

from FUNNY GIRL
Words by Bob Merrill
Music by Jule Styne

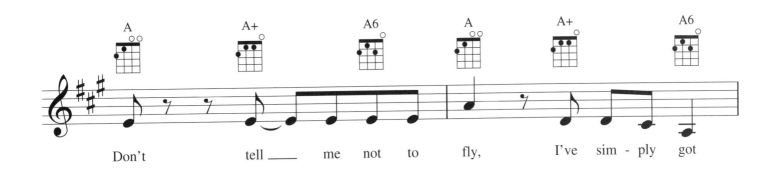

Don't tell ___ me not to fly, I've sim-ply got

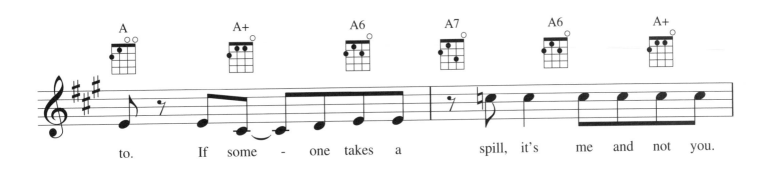

to. If some - one takes a spill, it's me and not you.

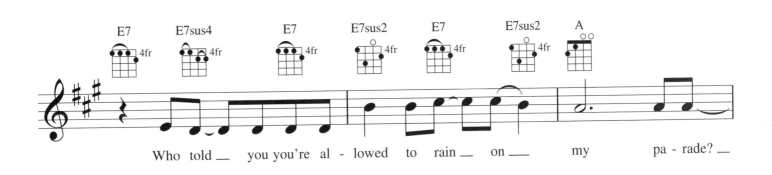

Who told ___ you you're al - lowed to rain ___ on ___ my pa - rade? ___

Chorus

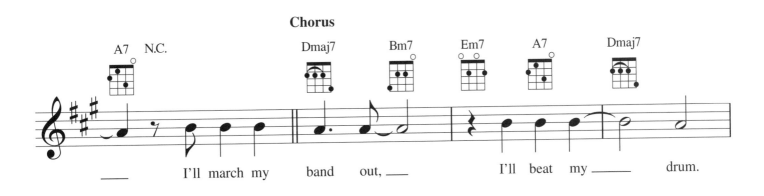

___ I'll march my band out, ___ I'll beat my ___ drum.

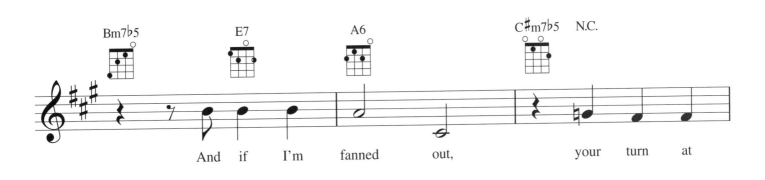

And if I'm fanned out, your turn at

bat,   sir, ____   at least I did - n't fake it.   Hat,   sir, ____   I

Verse

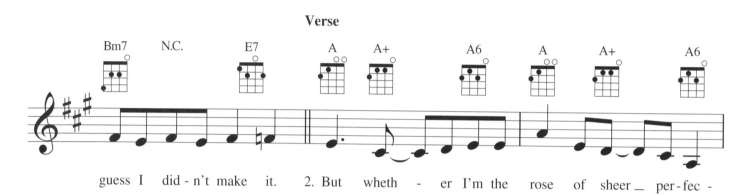

guess I did - n't make it.   2. But   wheth - er I'm the rose of sheer _ per - fec -

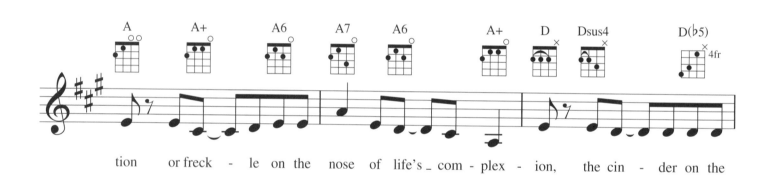

tion or freck - le on the nose of life's _ com - plex - ion,   the cin - der on the

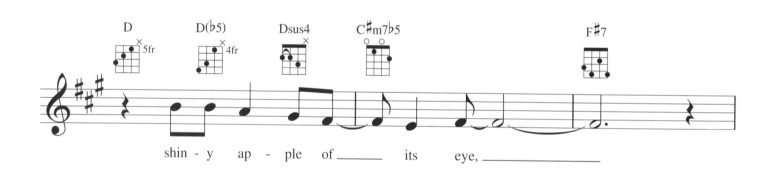

shin - y ap - ple of ____ its   eye, _____

I got - ta fly once, I ____ got - ta try once, on - ly can die once,

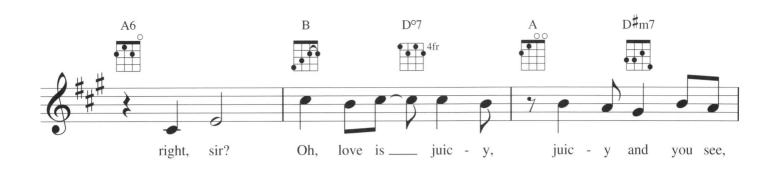

right, sir?　Oh, love is ___ juic - y,　juic - y and you see,

Verse

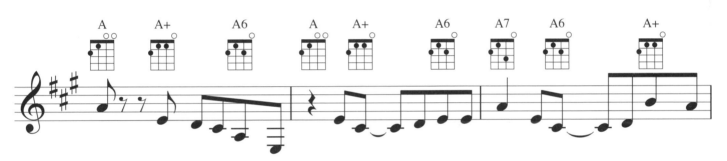

I got - ta have my bite, sir. ___　3. Get read - y for me,

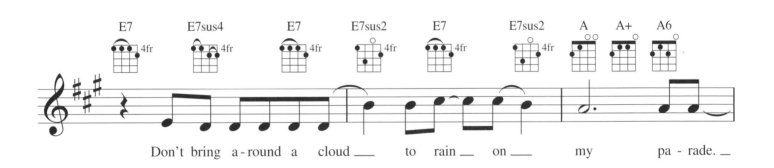

love, 'cause I'm a com - er.　I sim - ply got - ta march; my heart's ___ a drum - mer.

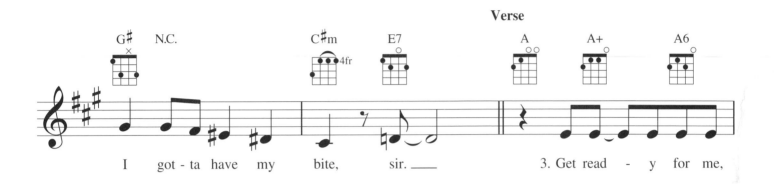

Don't bring a - round a cloud ___ to rain ___ on ___ my pa - rade. ___

Bridge

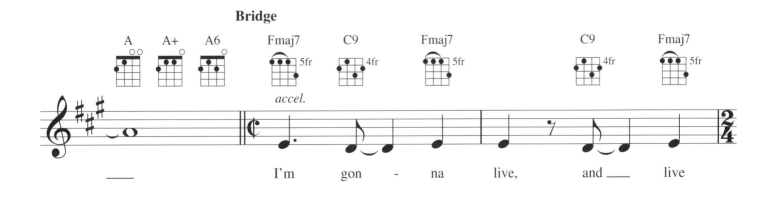

accel.

___　I'm gon - na live, and ___ live

now. Get what __ I want, I _____ know how.

One roll ___ for the whole _ she - bang.

One throw, _ that bell will ___ go clang.

Eye on _____ the tar - get ____ and wham!

One shot, __ one gun - shot ___ and bam!

Freely

Hey, Mis - ter Arn - stein, here

love, 'cause I'm __ a com - er.   I sim - ply got - ta march, my heart's __ a drum - mer.

Freely

No - bod - y, no, no - bod - y _____ is

gon - na _____ rain on my pa -

A Tempo

rade. _____

Hello

Words and Music by Lionel Richie

been a-lone with you in-side my _____ mind, _____ and
long to see the sun-light in your _____ hair _____ and
3. *Instrumental*

in my dreams I've kissed your lips a thou-sand times. I
tell you time and time a-gain how much I care. Some -

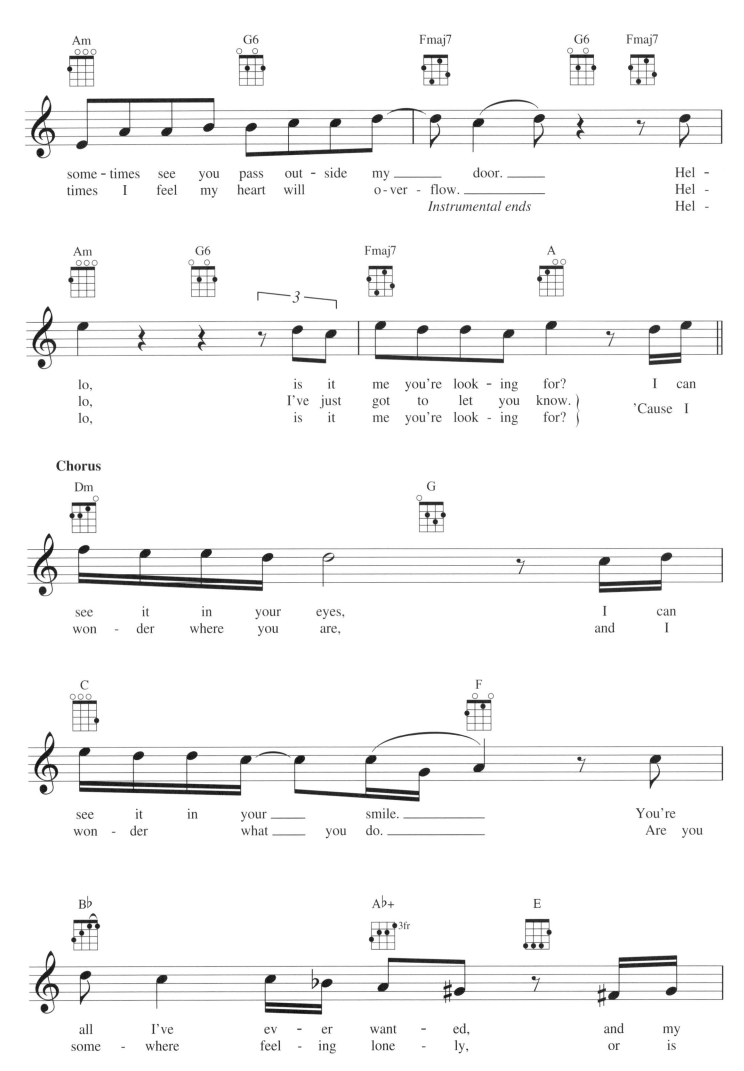

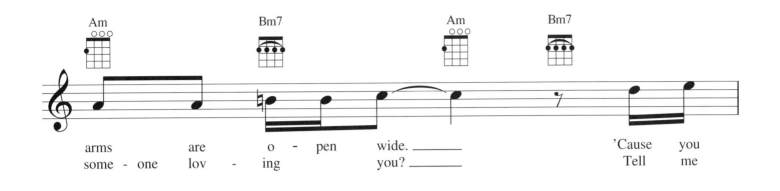

arms are o - pen wide. _____ 'Cause you
some - one lov - ing you? _____ Tell me

know just what to say, _____ and you know just what to do, ____ and I
how to win your _ heart for I have - n't got a clue, but

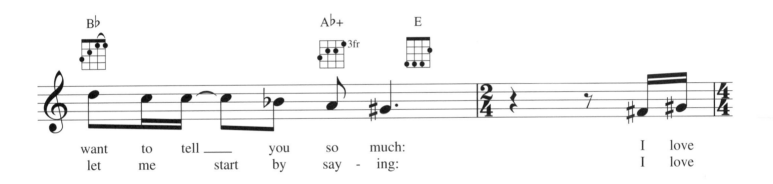

want to tell ____ you so much: I love
let me start by say - ing: I love

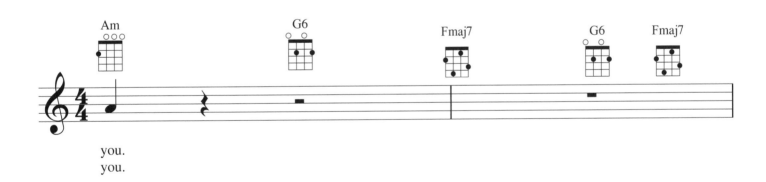

you.
you.

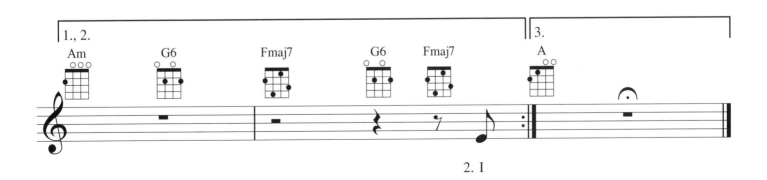

2. I

Don't Stop Believin'

Words and Music by Steve Perry, Neal Schon and Jonathan Cain

waiting ____

up and down the boul - e - vard, _ their

peo - ple, ___

liv - ing just to find e - mo - tion,

1.

shad - ows ___ search - ing ___ in the night. _____

hid - ing ___

2.

To Coda ⊕

some - where _ in the night. _____

Interlude

Verse

4. Work - ing hard _ to get my fill. ___

Ev - 'ry - bod - y

wants a thrill. _____

Pay - in' an - y - thing to

roll the dice ___ just one more ___ time. _____

⊕ Coda
Guitar Solo

Outro

Don't ___ stop be - liev - in'. Hold on to the

feel - in', _____ street - light

Repeat and fade

peo - ple. _____

Imagine

Words and Music by John Lennon

1. Im - ag - ine there's no heav - en, it's eas - y if you try; ___ ___ no hell ___ be - low us, a - bove us on - ly sky. ___ Im - ag - ine all the peo - ple ___ liv - ing for to - day, ___ ah. ___

Chorus

Additional Lyrics

3. Imagine no possessions,
   I wonder if you can;
   No need for greed or hunger,
   A brotherhood of man.
   Imagine all the people sharing all the world.

It's My Life

Words and Music by Jon Bon Jovi, Martin Sandberg and Richie Sambora

First note

Intro
Moderate Rock

Verse

1. This ain't a song — for the bro - ken - heart - ed.
2. *See additional lyrics*

No si - lent prayer — for faith de - part - ed.

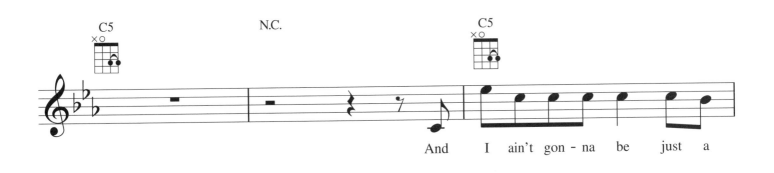

And I ain't gon - na be just a

face in the crowd. __ You're gon - na hear __ my voice when I

Chorus

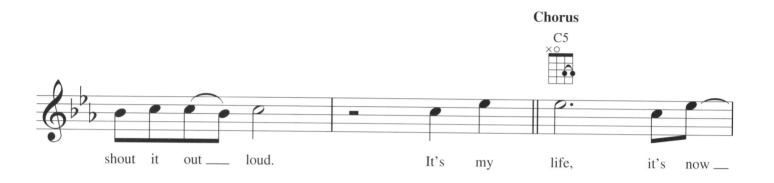

shout it out __ loud. It's my life, it's now __

__ or nev - er. Well, I ain't gon - na live for - ev - er.

I just wan - na live __ while I'm _____ a - live. ____

My heart is like an o - pen high - way. __

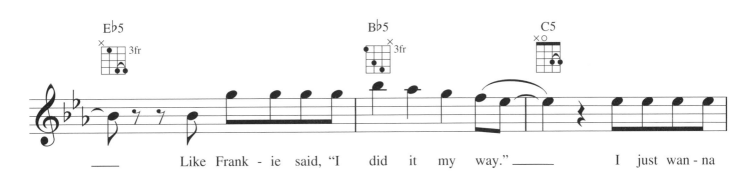

Like Frank - ie said, "I did it my way." _____ I just wan - na

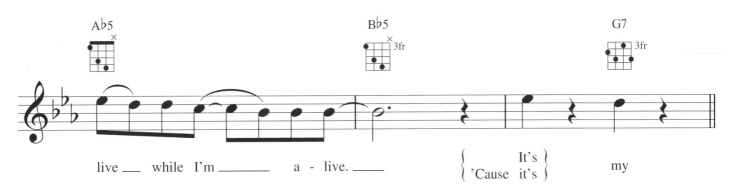

live _____ while I'm _____ a - live. _____ { It's / 'Cause it's } my

1.

Interlude

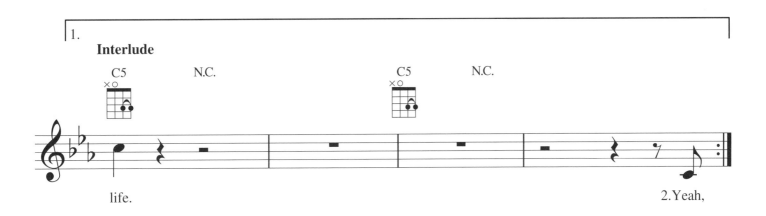

life. 2. Yeah,

2.

Guitar Solo

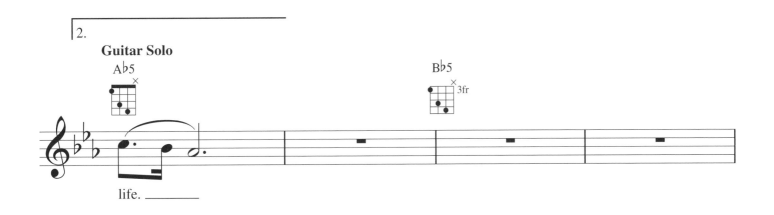

life. _____

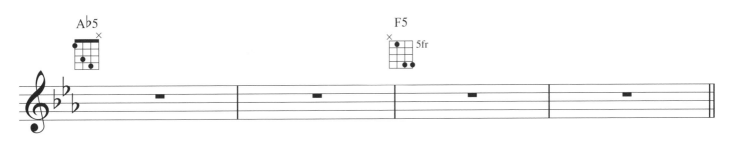

Bridge

Bet - ter stand tall when they're call - in' you out. ___ Don't bend, don't break, ba - by,

*Let chord ring, next 4 meas.

Outro-Chorus

don't back down. It's my { life, and } it's now ___
{ And }

___ or ___ nev - er. { 'Cause } I ain't gon - na live for - ev - er. ___

___ I just wan - na live ___ while I'm ___ a - live. ___

My heart is like an o - pen high - way.

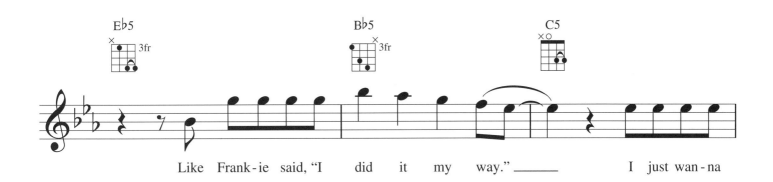

Like Frank-ie said, "I did it my way." _____ I just wan-na

1.

live ___ while I'm _____ a - live. ___

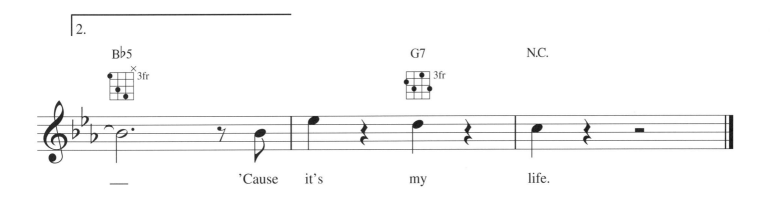

2.

__ 'Cause it's my life.

Additional Lyrics

2. Yeah, this is for the ones who stood their ground,
For Tommy and Gina, who never backed down.
Tomorrow's gettin' harder, make no mistake.
Luck ain't even lucky, gotta make your own breaks.

Jessie's Girl

Words and Music by Rick Springfield

1. Jes -

- sie is a friend,   yeah, I know _

2. *See additional lyrics*

_____ he's been a good friend of mine. _____   But late -

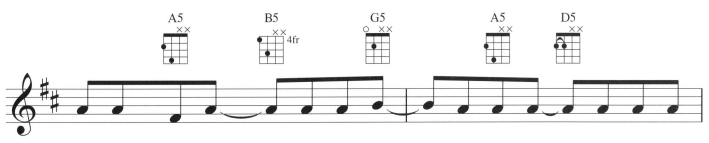

ly some - thing's changed; ___ it ain't hard _____ to de - fine. ___ Jes - sie's got

him - self a girl, ___ and I wan - na make her mine. ___ { And she's
{ 'Cause she's

Pre-Chorus

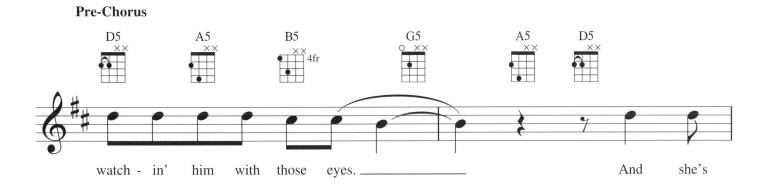

watch - in' him with those eyes. _____ And she's

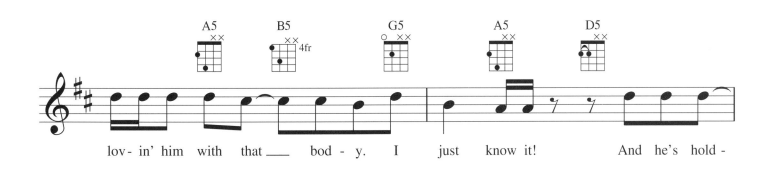

lov - in' him with that ___ bod - y. I just know it! And he's hold -

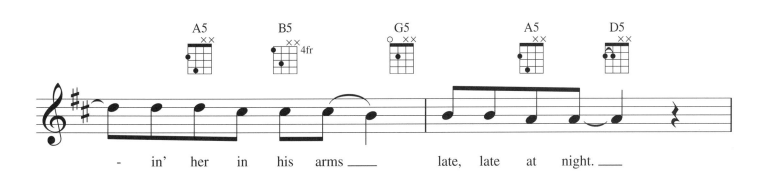

- in' her in his arms ___ late, late at night. ___

wom - an, where can I find a _____ wom - an like that?

Bridge

And I look in the mir - or all the time _____

won - d'rin' what she don't see _____ in me.

I've been fun - ny, I've been cool _____ with the lines. _____

Ain't that the way love's sup - posed _____ to be?

Interlude

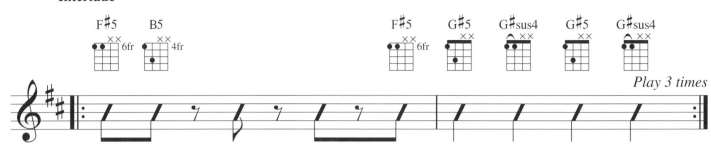

Play 3 times

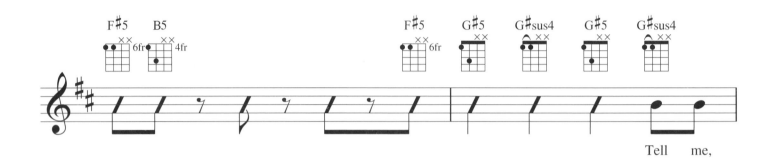

Tell me,

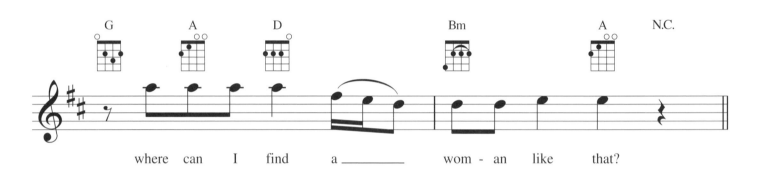

where can I find a _____ wom - an like that?

Guitar Solo

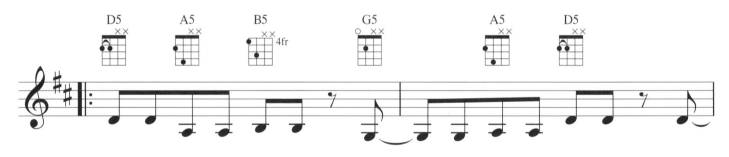

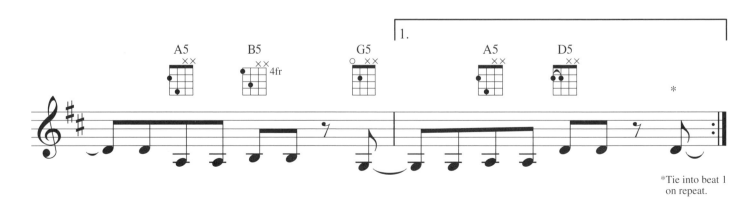

*Tie into beat 1
on repeat.

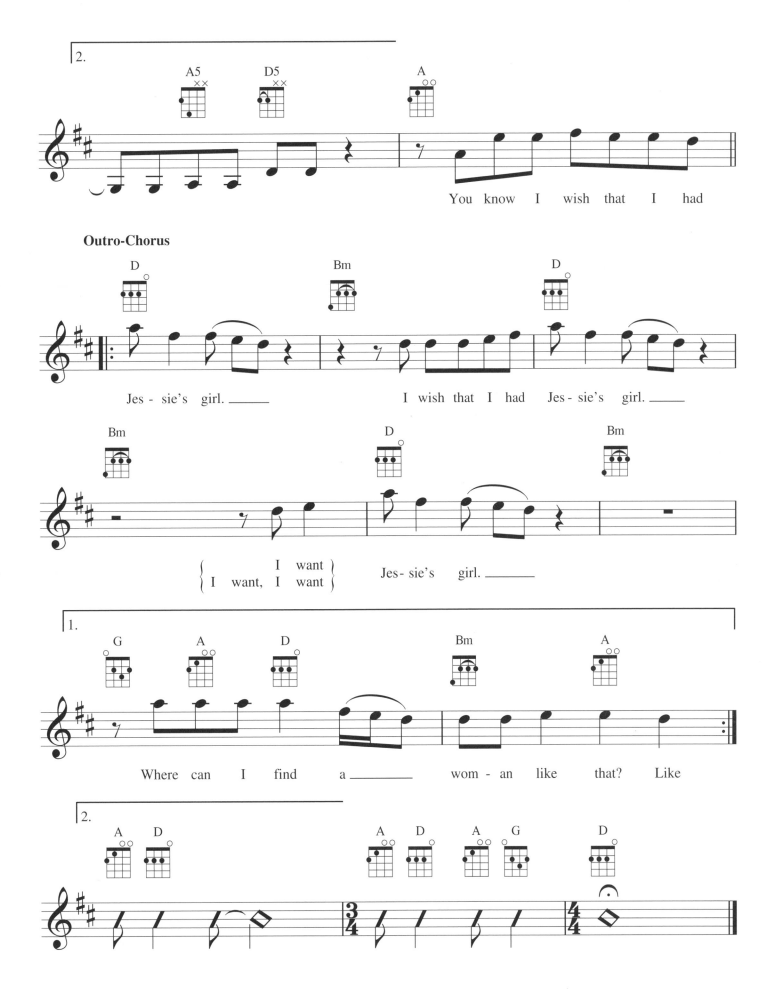

Outro-Chorus

Jes - sie's girl. _____   I wish that I had Jes - sie's girl. _____

{ I want, I want / I want } Jes - sie's girl. _____

You know I wish that I had

Where can I find a _____ wom - an like that? Like

Additional Lyrics

2. I'll play along with this charade.
   There doesn't seem to be a reason to change.
   You know, I feel so dirty when they start talkin' cute.
   I wanna tell her that I love her, but the point is prob'ly moot.

My Life Would Suck Without You

Words and Music by Lukasz Gottwald, Max Martin and Claude Kelly

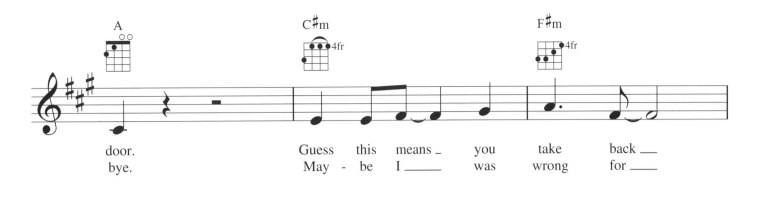

door.
bye.

Guess this means ___ you take back ___
May - be I ___ was wrong back for ___

all you said ___ be - fore,
try - in' to pick ___ a fight.

like how much ___ you
I know that I've ___ got

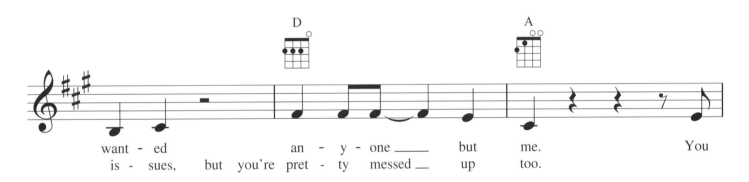

want - ed an - y - one ___ but me. You
is - sues, but you're pret - ty messed ___ up too.

said you'd nev - er come back, ___
Ei - ther way, ___ I found out ___

but here you are ___ a -
I'm noth - ing with - out

Chorus

gain.
you. _____

'Cause we be - long _____ to - geth -

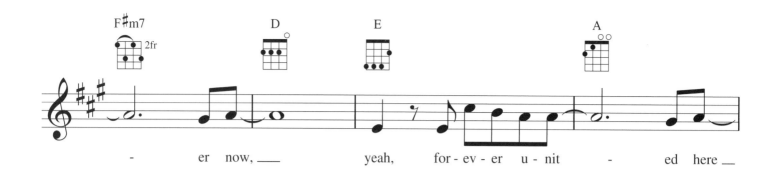

er now, ___ yeah, for - ev - er u - nit - ed here ___

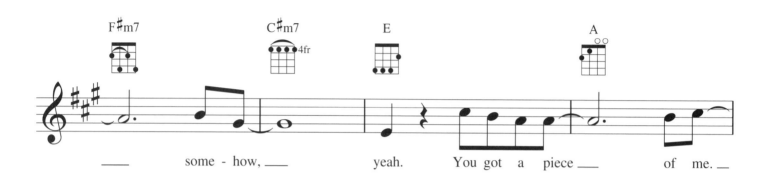

___ some - how, ___ yeah. You got a piece ___ of me. ___

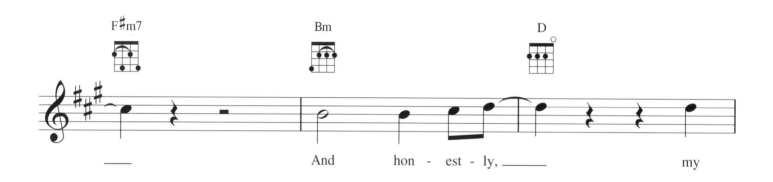

___ And hon - est - ly, _____ my

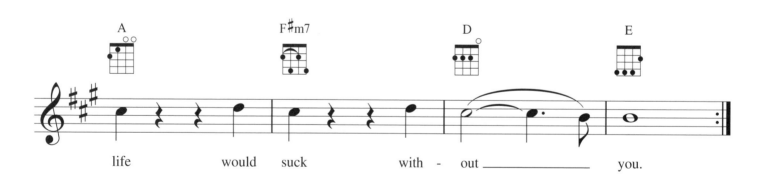

life would suck with - out _____ you.

Bridge

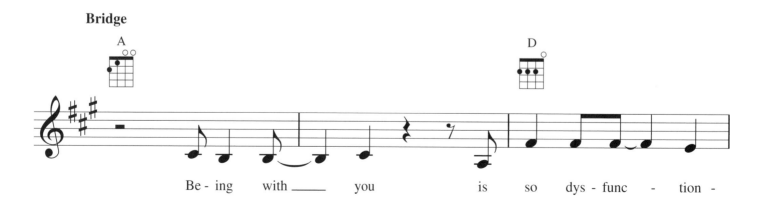

Be - ing with ___ you is so dys - func - tion -

al.   I   real - ly should - n't miss you, ___   but

Interlude

w/ Intro riff

I   can't let ___ you   go,   oh   yeah. ___

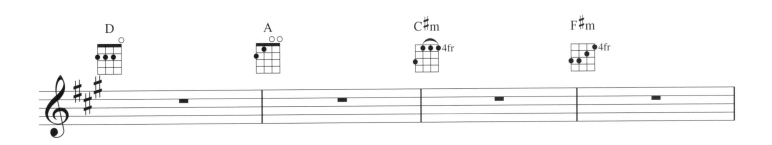

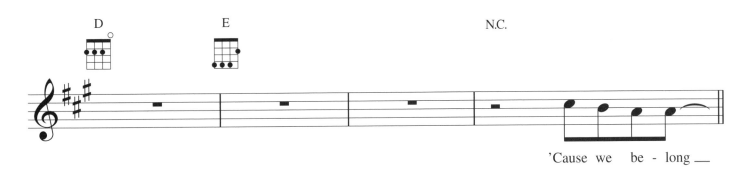

'Cause we be - long ___

Outro-Chorus

___   to - geth -   er now, _____

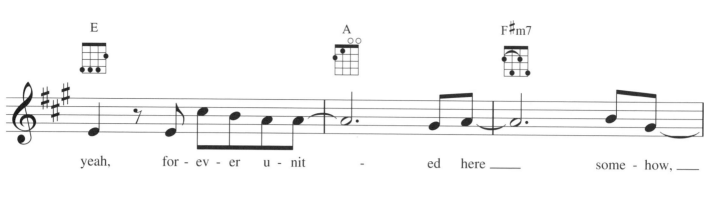

yeah, for - ev - er u - nit - ed here ____ some - how, ___

___ yeah. You got a piece ____ of me. __

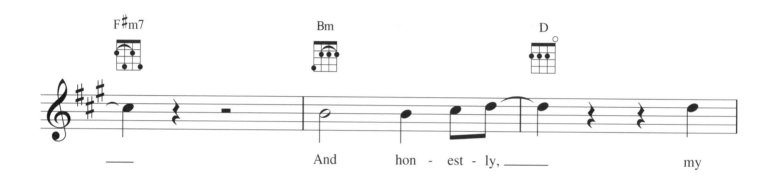

__ And hon - est - ly, _____ my

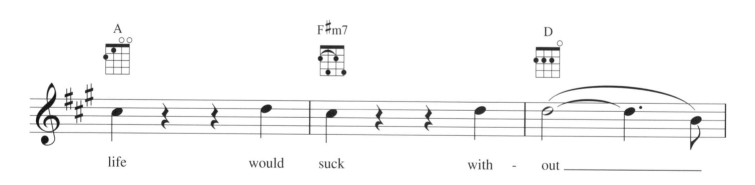

life would suck with - out _____

1.
you. 'Cause we be - long __
2.
you. _____

Rock and Roll All Nite

Words and Music by Paul Stanley and Gene Simmons

1. You show us ev - 'ry
2. You keep on say - in' you'll be

thing you've got. ___
mine for a - while. ___

You keep on danc - ing, and the
You're look - in' fan - cy, and I

room gets hot.
like your style.

You drive us wild; ___ we'll drive you cra -
And you drive us wild; ___ we'll drive you cra -

- zy. And you say you wan - na
- zy. And you show us ev - 'ry

go for a spin. ___   The par - ty's just be - gun; we'll
thing you've got.   Oh, ba - by, ba - by, that's

let you in.   You drive us wild; ___ we'll drive you cra -
quite a lot.   And you drive us wild; ___ we'll drive you cra -

Pre-Chorus

- zy.   You keep on shout - in', you ___
- zy.

___ keep on shout - in'.   I ___

Chorus

___ wan - na rock and roll ___ all night ___

and par - ty ev - er - ry day.   I wan - na rock and roll ___ all night ___

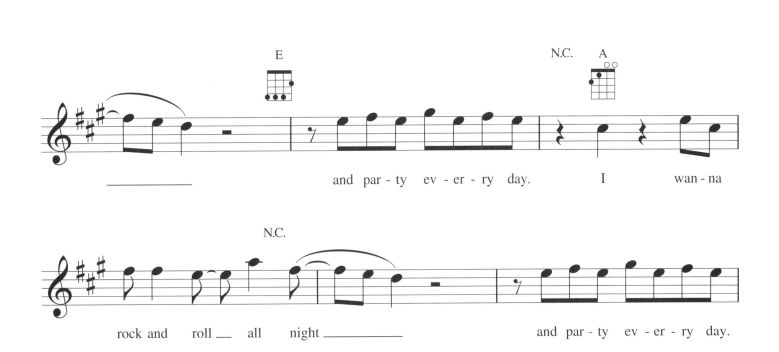

and par - ty ev - er - ry day.   I   wan - na

rock and roll ___ all night _____   and par - ty ev - er - ry day.

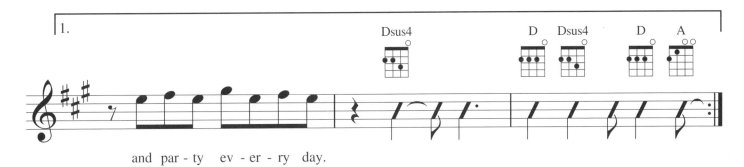

I   wan - na   rock and   roll ___ all   night _____

1.

and par - ty ev - er - ry day.

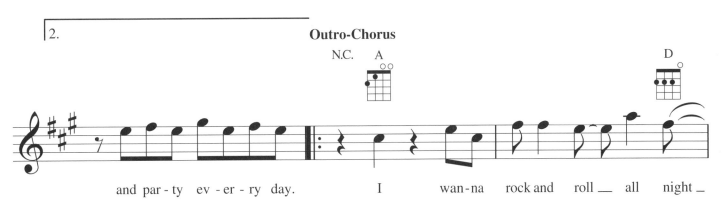

2.   **Outro-Chorus**

and par - ty ev - er - ry day.   I   wan - na rock and   roll ___ all   night _

Repeat and fade

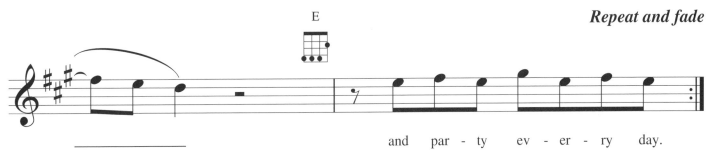

and par - ty ev - er - ry day.

No Air

Words and Music by James Fauntleroy II, Steven Russell, Harvey Mason, Jr., Damon Thomas and Erik Griggs

Los - ing you was like liv - ing in a world with no ____ air, ____
There's no grav - i - ty to hold me down __ for real. _____

oh, ___ oo. _____ *Male:* I'm here a - lone, did - n't want to leave. __
Female: But some - how I'm still a - live __ in - side. __

My heart won't move, __ it's in - com - plete. Wish there was a way
You took my breath, __ but I sur - vived. I don't know how, __

that I could make you un - der - stand. _____
but I don't e - ven care. _____

Female: But
Both: So

Pre-Chorus

how do you ___ ex - pect me _____ to

live a - lone __ with just me? ___ 'Cause my world re - volves ___ a -

No air, ___ air. ___ No air, ___ air. ___

No air, ___ air. ___ No air, ___ air. ___

Interlude

There's no air, no air. ___

Oh, oh. ___

Outro-Chorus

Tell me how I'm s'posed to breathe with no air. _____ Can't

live, can't breathe with no air. _____ That's how I feel when-ev-er you ain't

there. _____ There's no air, no air. _____ { Both: / Female: } Got me

out here in the wa-ter so deep. { Both: / Male: } Tell me how you gon' be with-out

me? { Both: / Female: } If you ain't here, I just can't breathe. _ *Both:* There's no

Over the Rainbow

from THE WIZARD OF OZ

Lyric by E.Y. "Yip" Harburg

Music by Harold Arlen

there's a land that ___ I dreamed of ___

heard

once in ___ a lull - a - by, _____

Verse

hy. _____ 2. Oh, some - where

o - ver ___ the rain - bow ___ skies ___ are

blue, and the

dreams that ___ you dare to dream real - ly do come

true, _____

hoo. _____

Guitar Solo

_____

Bridge

day I'll wish _ up - on a star _ and wake up where the clouds _ are far be -

hind.   me. _____   Where trou - bles melt _ like

Oh,   some -

Proud Mary

Words and Music by John Fogerty

First note

Intro
Moderate Rock

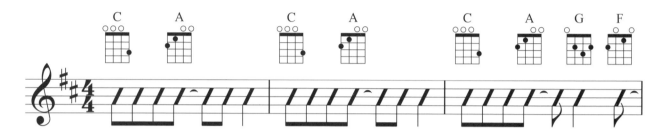

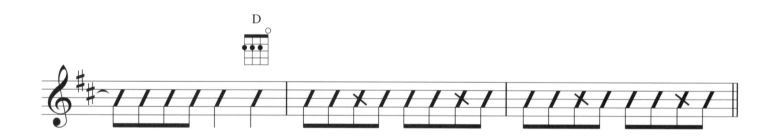

Verse

1. Left a good job __ in the cit - y, work - in' for the man __ ev -'ry
2., 4. *See additional lyrics*
3. *Instrumental*

night and day, __ and I nev - er lost __ one min - ute of sleep - in'

wor - ry - in' 'bout the way ___ things might have been. ___

Chorus

1., 2., 4. Big wheel ___ keep on turn - in',   Proud Mar - y keep on burn -
3. *Instrumental*

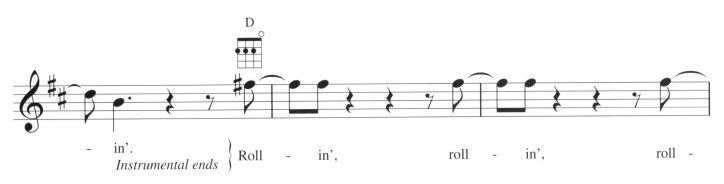

- in'.   *Instrumental ends* } Roll - in',   roll - in',   roll -

4th time, To Coda ⊕   **2nd time, D.C**
                 3rd time, D.C. al Coda   ⊕ **Coda**

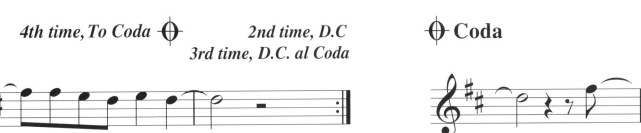

- in' on the riv - er. ___   ___ Roll -

Outro
                                                   Repeat and fade

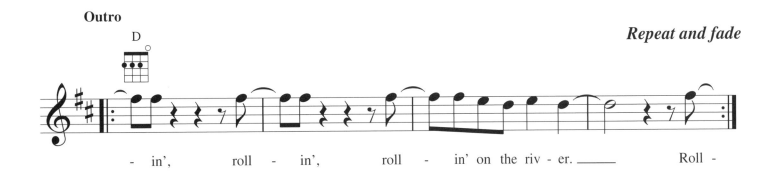

- in',   roll - in',   roll - in' on the riv - er. ___   Roll -

Additional Lyrics

2. Cleaned a lot of plates in Memphis,
   Pumped a lot of pain in New Orleans,
   But I never saw the good side of the city,
   Until I hitched a ride on a river boat queen.

4. If you come down to the river,
   Bet you gonna find some people who live.
   You don't have to worry 'cause you have no money.
   People on the river are happy to give.

Rehab

Words and Music by Amy Winehouse

First note

Chorus
Moderately fast

They tried to make me go to re - hab, __ I __ said,

"No, __ no, __ no." __ Yes, __ I been __ black, but when __

__ I come __ back, you won't know, __ know, __ know. __

I ain't got the time, __ and if my dad - dy __ thinks __ I'm

fine, ___ he's tried to make me go to re - hab, __ I ___ won't ___

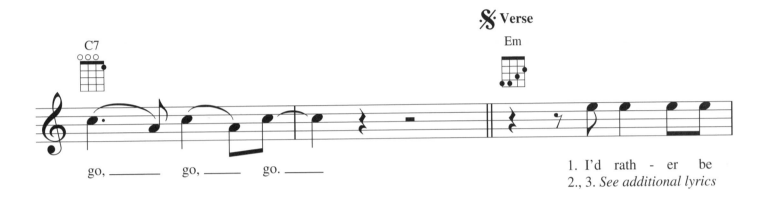

Verse

go, _____ go, _____ go. _____

1. I'd rath - er be
2., 3. *See additional lyrics*

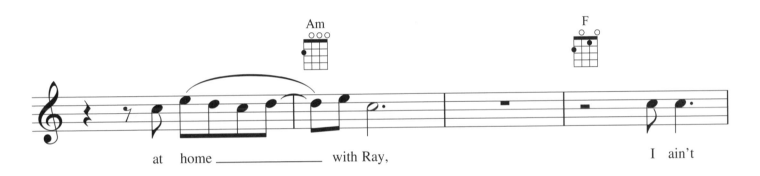

at home _____ with Ray, I ain't

got sev - en - ty days. _____ 'Cause there's

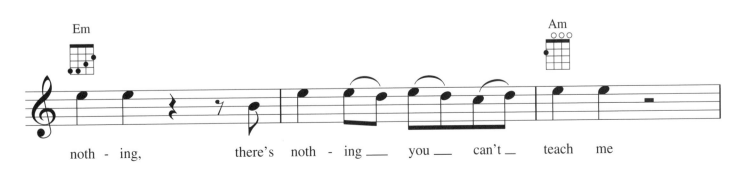

noth - ing, there's noth - ing ___ you ___ can't ___ teach me

that   I   can't   learn __   from   Mis - ter

Hath - a - way. _____   I   did - n't

get   a   lot   in   class, ___   but   I

know   it   don't   come   in   a   shot   glass.   They

Chorus

tried   to   make   me   go   to   re - hab, ___   I ___ said, ___

"No, ___ no, ___ no." ___   Yes, ___ I   been _ black, but when _

_____ I come _ back, you won't know, _____ know, _ know. _____

⊕ **Coda**

_____ I ain't got the time, _____ and if my

dad - dy _ thinks _ I'm fine, _ he's tried to make me go to re -

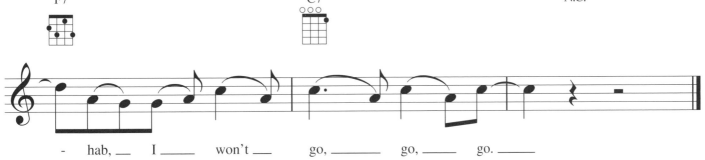

- hab, _ I _____ won't _ go, _____ go, _____ go. _____

Additional Lyrics

2. The man said, "Why do you think you're here?"
   I said, "I got no idea.
   I'm gonna, I'm gonna lose my baby,
   So I always keep a bottle near."
   He said, "I just think you're depressed,
   Kiss me, baby, and go rest."

3. I don't ever want to drink again.
   I just, ooh I just need a friend.
   I'm not gonna spend ten weeks,
   Have everyone think I'm on the mend.
   It's not just my pride,
   It's just 'til these tears have dried.

Somebody to Love

Words and Music by Freddie Mercury

hard - earned pay ___ all ___ on my own. I go down on my knees, and I ___

To Coda ⊕

___ start to pray ___ 'til the tears run down from my eyes, Lord.

Chorus

Some - bod - y, oo, some - bod - y, can an - y - bod - y find me ___

___ some - bod - y to love? ___

Bridge

Ev - 'ry day I've tried, and I've tried, and I've tried, ___ but

ev - 'ry bod - y wants to put me down. ___ They say I'm go'n' cra -

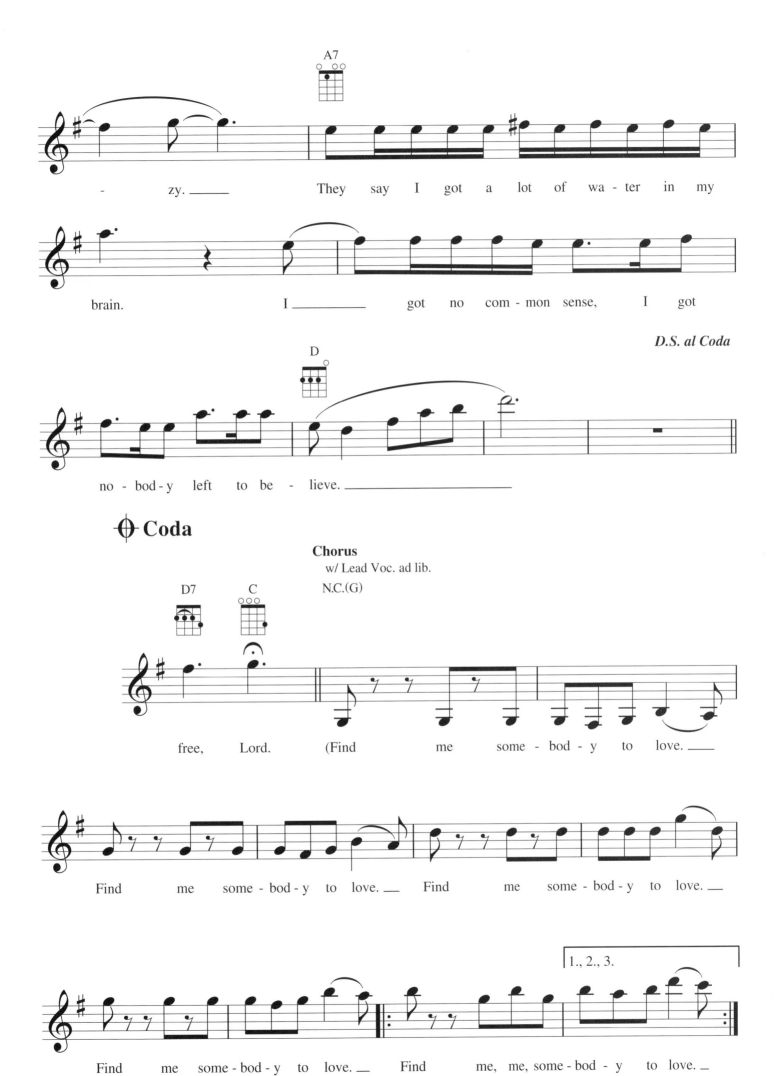

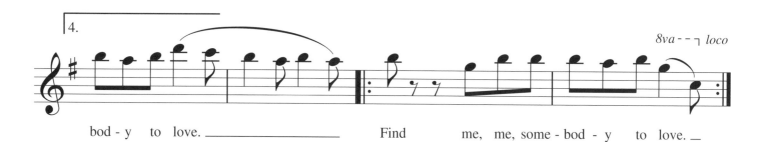

bod - y   to   love. _____   Find   me, me, some - bod - y   to   love. _

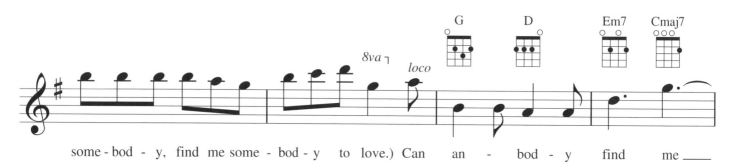

Some - bod   -   y,   some - bod   -   y,   some - bod   -   y,   some - bod   -   y,   some - bod   -   y,   find   me

some - bod - y,   find me some - bod - y   to   love.)   Can   an   -   bod   -   y   find   me ____

Freely

_____   some - bod - y   to ____   love? _____

Outro

w/ Lead Voc. ad lib.

A Tempo

Repeat and fade

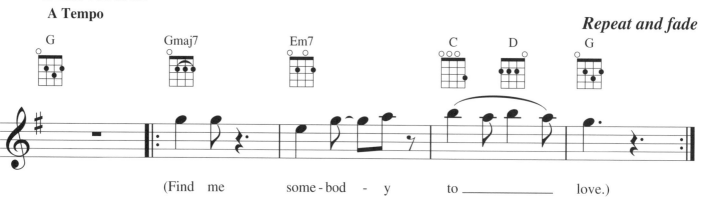

(Find   me   some - bod   -   y   to _____   love.)

Additional Lyrics

4. Got no feel, I got no rhythm,
   I'll just keep losing my beat.
   I'm O.K., I'm alright.
   I ain't gonna face no defeat.
   I just gotta get out of this prison cell,
   Someday I'm gonna be free, Lord.

Sweet Caroline

Words and Music by Neil Diamond

came the sum - mer.
off my shoul - ders.
Who'd have be - lieved ___ you'd come ___ a - long? ___
How can I hurt ___ when hold - in' you? ___

___
___
Pre-Chorus
Hands, ___
Warm, ___

touch - in' hands, ___
touch - in' warm, ___
reach - in' out,

touch - in' me,
touch - in' you. ___

Chorus

Sweet Car - o - line, ___ good times nev - er seemed ___ so

good.
I've been in - clined ___

to be - lieve ___ they nev - er would. ___ 2. But now I

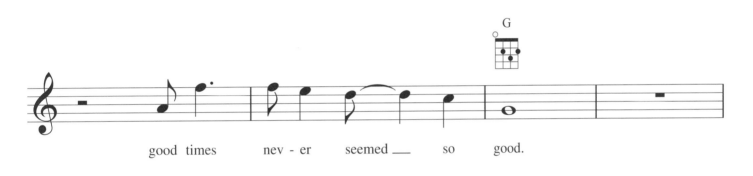

D.C. al Coda

⊕ **Coda**

___ Oh, no, no.

Outro-Chorus

Sweet Car - o - line, ___

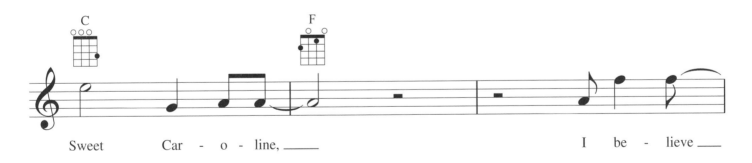

good times nev - er seemed ___ so good.

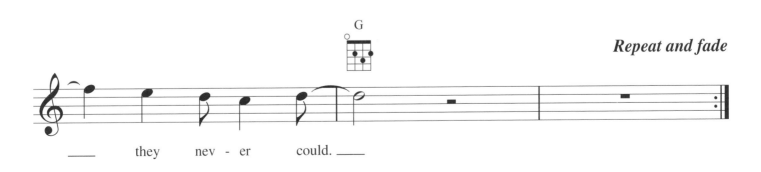

Sweet Car - o - line, ___ I be - lieve ___

Repeat and fade

___ they nev - er could. ___

Take a Bow

Words and Music by Shaffer Smith, Tor Erik Hermansen and Mikkel Eriksen

First note

Intro
Moderately

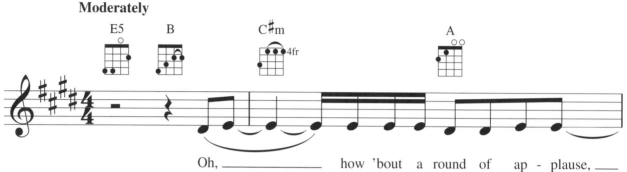

Oh, _____ how 'bout a round of ap - plause, _____

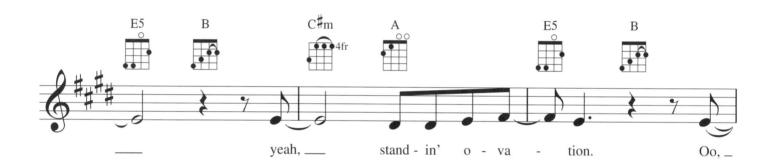

_____ yeah, _____ stand - in' o - va - tion. Oo, _____

_____ oh, _____ yeah. _____ Yeah, yeah, yeah, yeah.

Verse

1. You look so dumb right now _____
2. Grab your clothes and get gone, _____ you bet - ter hur - ry up

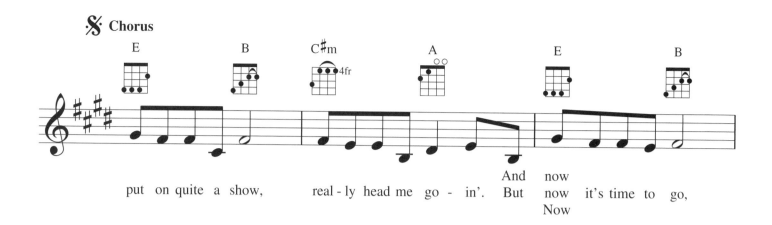

put on quite a show, real - ly head me go - in'. But now it's time to go,
And now
Now

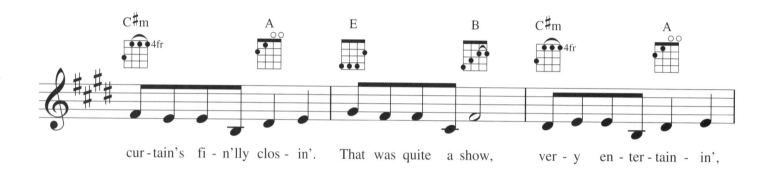

cur - tain's fi - n'lly clos - in'. That was quite a show, ver - y en - ter - tain - in',

To Coda ⊕

but it's o - ver now. ____ (But it's o - ver now.) Go on and take __ a bow, __

Bridge

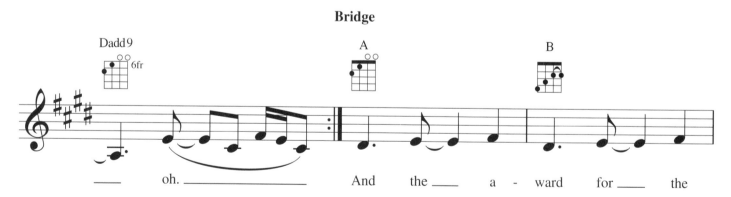

____ oh. _____ And the ___ a - ward for ___ the

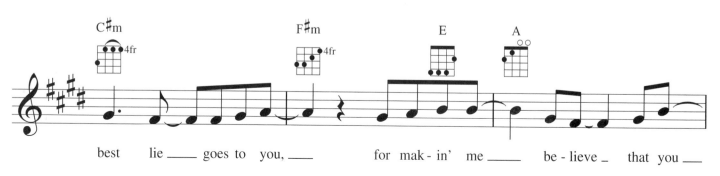

best lie ___ goes to you, ___ for mak - in' me ____ be - lieve _ that you ___

___ could be ___ faith - ful ___ to me. __ Let's hear ___ your speech, oh. _____

Pre-Chorus

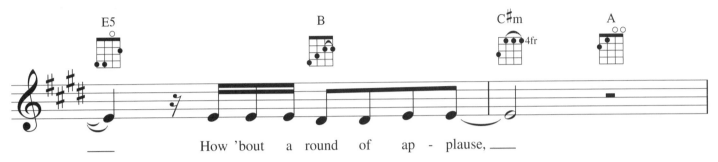

___ How 'bout a round of ap - plause, ____

D.S. al Coda

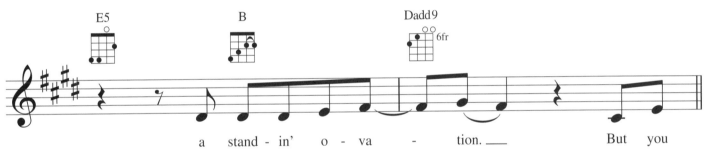

_a stand - in' o - va - tion. __ But you_

⊕ Coda

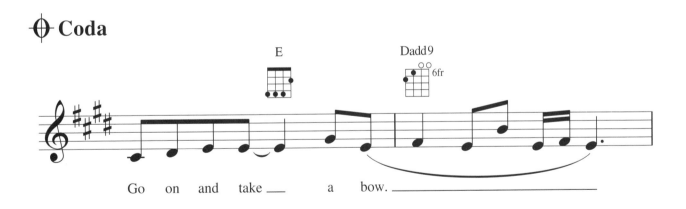

_Go on and take __ a bow. _____

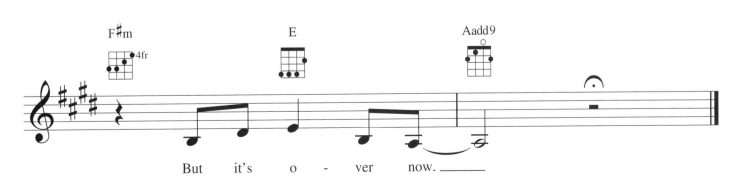

_But it's o - ver now. ____

Total Eclipse of the Heart

Words and Music by Jim Steinman

best of all the years have gone by. ___   Ev -'ry now and then I get a
Turn a - round.) ___

lit - tle bit ter - ri - fied, and then I see the look in your eyes. ___

Pre-Chorus

(Turn a - round, ___ bright ___ eyes.   Ev -'ry now and then I fall a -

part.
Turn a - round, ___ bright ___ eyes.)   Ev -'ry now and then I fall a -

Chorus

part, and I need you now ___ to - night; and I

need you more ___ than ev - er. And if you on - ly hold ___ me tight,

To Coda

Refrain

for-ev - er's gon-na start _ to - {night.}{Once} up-on a time I was

*Sung at once.

fall-ing in love, _ but now I'm on-ly fall-ing a - part. _

There's noth-ing I can do, a to-tal e-clipse _ of the heart. _

Once up-on a time there was light in my life, but now there's on-ly love in the dark.

Noth-ing I can say, a to-tal e-clipse _ of the heart. _

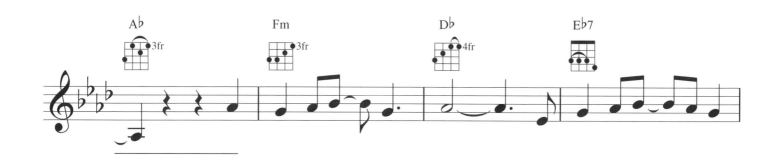

D.S. al Coda

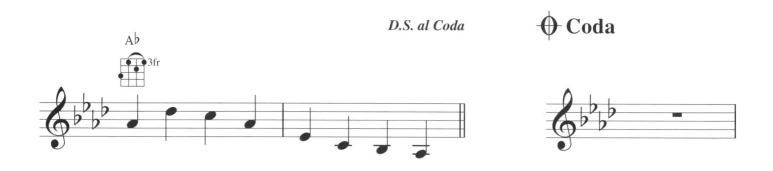

$\oplus$ **Coda**

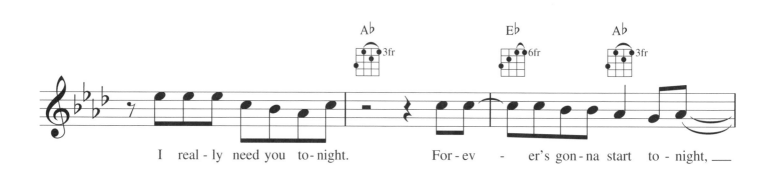

I real - ly need you to - night. For - ev - er's gon - na start to - night, ___

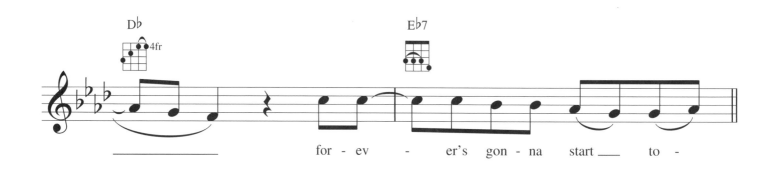

___ for - ev - er's gon - na start ___ to -

Outro-Refrain

{ night. / Once } up - on a time I was fall - ing in love, but now I'm on - ly fall - ing a - part.

*Sung at once.

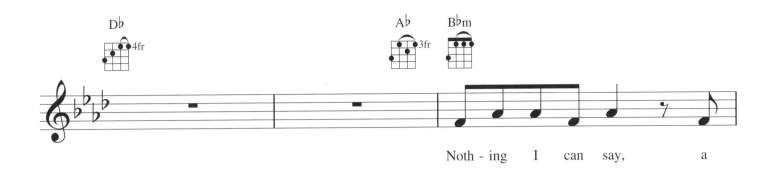

Noth - ing I can say, a

to - tal e - clipse ___ of the heart, ___

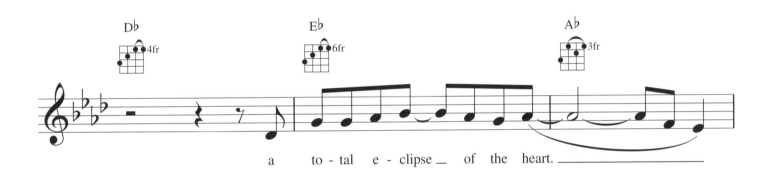

a to - tal e - clipse ___ of the heart. _____

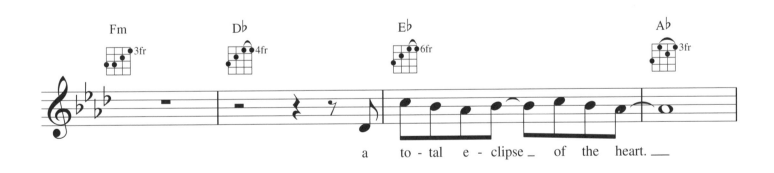

a to - tal e - clipse ___ of the heart. __

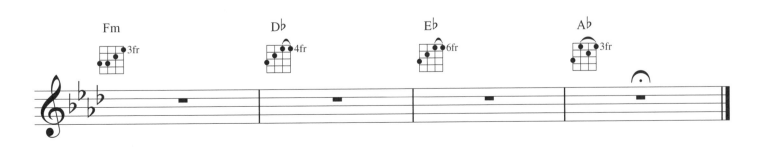

True Colors

Words and Music by Billy Steinberg and Tom Kelly

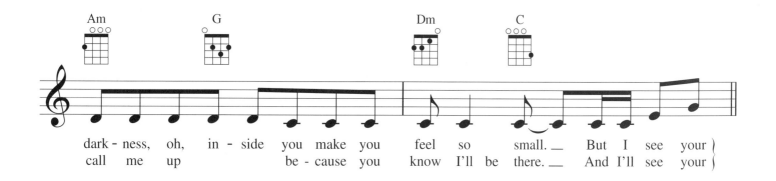

dark - ness, oh, in - side you make you feel so small. __ But I see your
call me up be - cause you know I'll be there. __ And I'll see your

Chorus

true col - ors shin - ing through. { 1. I / 2., 3. I'll } see your true col - ors, and

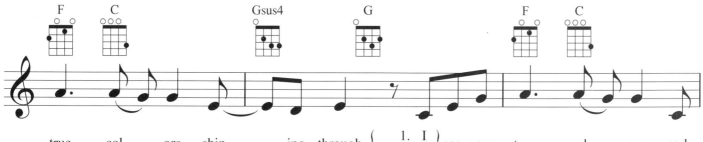

that's why I love _____ you. So don't be a - fraid _____ to { 1. let them show __ me your / 2., 3. let it show. _____ Your }

To Coda ⊕

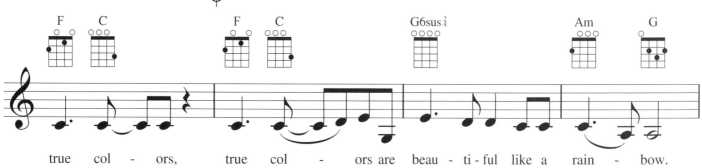

true col - ors, true col - ors are beau - ti - ful like a rain - bow.

1.   2.

D.S. al Coda

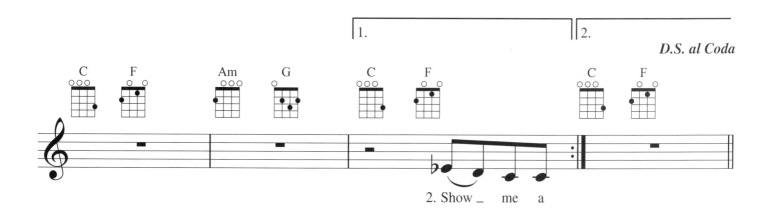

2. Show __ me a

Coda

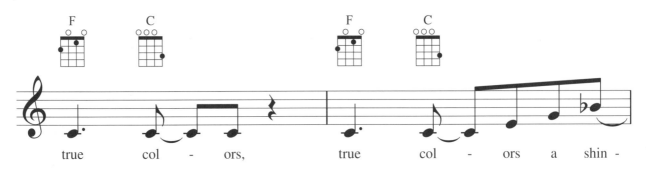

true col - ors, true col - ors a shin -

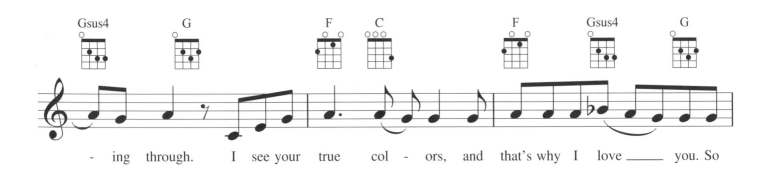

- ing through. I see your true col - ors, and that's why I love _____ you. So

rit.

don't be a - fraid _ to let them show. _____ Your true col - ors,

Freely

true col - ors are beau - ti - ful like a rain - bow. _

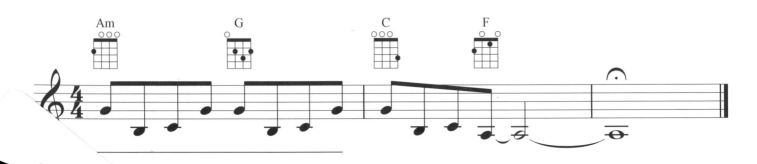